Building with Logs

B. Allan Mackie

Charles Scribner's Sons
New York, New York

Building with Logs
© Canada, 1979, Seventh Edition
Log House Publishing Company Ltd.

1st published 1971, revised 1979 in Canada by
Log House Publishing Co.
of Prince George, British Columbia

Reprinted 1972, 1973, 1974, 1975, 1976, 1977, 1979, 1980

U.S. edition published by
Charles Scribner's Sons 1981

Copywritten under the
Berne Convention

1 3 5 7 9 11 13 15 17 19   I/C   20 18 16 14 12   10 8 6 4 2

Printed in Canada

Library of Congress Catalogue
Card Number 80-53966
ISBN Number 0-684-16959-2

Table of Contents

"...(Arthur Erickson) became more and more aware of historical tradition and increasingly began to distrust false inventiveness in new buildings and the use of new technological methods merely for the sake of technology. 'The past,' he notes, 'was responsible for some courageous buildings compared with the timidity of today'."

— p. 261, *Canadian Architecture 1960/1970.*

From the beginning
there have been
courageous log buildings
in Canada.

Samuel de Champlain's men
at Port Royal in 1605
used solid timber
and built magnificently. . .

The Jesuits
at Midlands, 1639,
built the mission in solid timber
to a scale and exactitude
that astonished archaeologists
of the 20th century.

Hudson's Bay Company
heavy timber trading posts
throughout the West
still mark
the log building tradition.

John Moberly, HBC factor,
wrote in *When Fur Was King*
of substantial log houses
of the first settlers.

Many Canadians grew up in
log homes.

". . . then rose the Log House
by the water side"
wrote Joseph Howe
in his poem, "Acadia", 1874.

And the census of 1821 found
⅔ of all Ontario homes
(28,571) were log.

Many of these Canadians
were famous,
and told about their homes,
or biographers
recorded how they were.

Laura Secord's father in 1795
built a log house
at Oxford Township, site of
the town of Ingersoll, Ontario.

Cedar logs
made the boyhood home
in Egypt, Ontario,
of Stephen Leacock.

". . . beside
the curving trail
from Saint-Boniface

lay the family home . . .
plain, square-timbered,
with a steep-pitched roof . . .
for all its simplicity
a well-built little house",
the home of Louis Riel.

Nellie McClung
describes
all three of the family homes,
one in Ontario,
then, near Brandon, Manitoba
a quick one and, next winter, a
permanent home
all of "dressed timber
and whitewashed . . ."
In 1882 "we built our house:
logs
had been brought
for two winters
from the bush,
squared
and made ready. . . .
and there came a great day
when the neighbours gathered
to raise the building.
A long table was set
in the shadow of the old house,
roast chicken, potatoes, turnips,
custard pie, currant buns,

and big pots of tea
cheered the workers. . . .
That house was a great joy to us,
with a big room downstairs, a
bedroom for father and mother, a
large kitchen and pantry,
real stairs,
and two bedrooms above.
It still stands (1935),
a little bent
with the heaviness of years . . . ."

There is
a W. L. Mackenzie King
log house
in Saskatchewan.

The largest log building
in the world is
at Montebello, Quebec.
An elegant C.P.R. hotel, it
was built in 1930
of British Columbia red cedar.

And to-day there are
three professional log
builder associations:
Western Canada,
Ontario and Quebec.

BUILDING WITH LOGS

in the 7th edition

is dedicated to those gallant Canadians who dare to continue this fine tradition of log building.

The axeman

in the twentieth century

displaying this determination

to find peace

and sanity

is joined in history

to every pioneer

who set himself to carving

a homestead

in a new world.

Many Canadians think of themselves as natural born axemen. Indeed, they are entitled to this image even though they may never have seen a tree felled, for it is still possible in this country to develop, with pride, these skills which were practised by our surprisingly recent ancestors.

This book was intended, originally, to encourage those Canadians who would leave the suburban reservations to live part of their lives at peace with nature. Over the years, this book has reached a far wider audience so that now, in its 7th edition, it is addressed to all those throughout the world who admire solid timber construction as one of the strongest, most durable and beautiful building forms known.

There are three prime reasons for using natural logs in construction. First, a log house is one of the most aesthetically satisfying in which to live. Logs bring the world of nature back into our lives in a way that becomes ever more necessary to our survival. There is a deep sense of peace, living in a house made of natural trees. No stripped, chipped, cooked, treated, compressed, or otherwise manufactured product of industrial technology can give such an awareness of each living tree, just as it once stood. You, as builder, will remember long after your house is finished, whether a tree had few limbs or many because of where it grew. You'll know how it looked as it fell to the ground. A scar may remind you of the day the logs were skidded to the building site. The length of time it took you to build will be recorded in the faint darkening of the rising logs as they became drier and less easy to peel. You will remember a log that chased you down the skids or one that humped its

back before it was subdued and fitted into place. The scrubbing, oiling, and perhaps varnishing will warm the colours and highlight the textures of the new walls ... revealing curves, limb lines, the lacework of bark beetles or the clawmarks of a bear ... all signs of nature to be saved and treasured. Finally, there is a growing understanding of all vegetation having consciousness. I accept that view. And I believe it accounts for that intense feeling of peace and thankfulness which permeates a natural, carefully-built log home. I leave it with the reader to consider what response the living spirit of a tree must feel when put to rest as part of your well-loved household.

The family that builds a log house knows their home as a work of art. They can savour it as no other. None but the log house provides its own sweet incense of sap and resin. Solid timber walls have an acoustic quality that makes music sound richer. Harsh household clatter does not strike, echo, and bounce as it does from plaster surfaces. The natural brown tones are restful to the eye. Above all, there is a quality of snug security in the fortress-thick walls. This may come from tradition, log construction being old and honoured in Canadian history. A log building ties that time tested tradition into our uncertain todays, giving a welcome sense of continuity and stability.

The second advantage of log construction is durability. With a good foundation to protect the wood from the composting urge of earth, and a wide overhang to shelter against rain and snow soakings, the log building will rival concrete in its long life. In style, the log house has an amazing durability. The pressures of fashion have never succeeded in making a log building look outdated. It is in timeless

good taste whether a simple building or the dramatic 20th century designs. Logs have an innate harmony with the landscape as long as they are used with dignity and with care.

Third: log construction is the only contemporary construction method which enables an individual to exchange labour and ingenuity, rather than cash or a mortgage indebtness, for a home to be proud of. Building with logs does require hard work; but it is healthy, pleasant work which is not at all beyond the strength of most families if it is undertaken at a pace that permits full appreciation of the undertaking as a once-in-a-lifetime experience. Our first home of only 700 square feet, on the shores of Francois Lake, was built in 1953 for a total cash outlay of two hundred dollars. The only purchased items were glass, roofing, spar varnish, and rough lumber. The rest was accomplished with a good deal of innovating, trading, scrounging, and neighbourly cooperation ... all activities which are still permissible in many parts of this country. But where the use of logs as building material requires not only the purchase and delivery of all materials but also the hiring of the builders, the log house will be as costly as frame or masonry construction. This should not deter the family able to afford what pleases them most. And savings will occur both in heating and airconditioning as well as in the low cost of building maintenance over the centuries.

So let us begin the discussion of how to build with logs knowing this to be a discussion, for there are always different ways to do each task. Every axeman will find many new answers of his own. This is part of the craft. It is what helps to make each house unique ... a work of art.

The tree, as building material

I am going to ask that this discussion on log building construction begin with a close look at the tree as it stands in nature, before a hand is laid upon it. Many of us have two hang-ups about trees: agrarian and cultural. In the agrarian past, the tree was an enemy. It constantly threatened to invade pastures and fields or it was already using land which could otherwise provide food crops. The farmer waged a constant war to eradicate trees from his holdings and, in the past, it was more of an equal battle. But with the coming of the bulldozer, farmers gained the upper hand. Never again would he need to fear that the forest would reclaim his land. The agrarian instinct was not calmed, however. People rushed headlong about the landscape fighting the war against nature, toppling trees and heaping them up for burning just as rubbish is burned. The joy of victory carried us ever onward, clearing and breaking much forest land which should never have been expected to grow anything else but timber. The ancestral urge for land is not an easy instinct to curb. And often I wonder if this urge resurfaces in the urbanized setting as an unthinking contempt for trees, as of yore. But that's only one hang-up. The other I've called cultural for industrial sales have helped reshape our values away from natural shapes and textures and toward an appreciation of a "finished" product. We've learned to distrust the possibility that one of life's necessities could be found perfect in nature. Food, one might suppose, grows in supermarkets. And then they began to wax

the turnips, thinking they'd look better when they appeared in the store. And so, with this same mixed training in realism, some people approach the building of a log house feeling that the tree, as it is found in nature, is not quite good enough; that it should have (as a longtime logger said to me) "some kind of finish".

A close look at the tree's physical properties will help overcome both these hang-ups. First, the body of the tree is composed of hollow cells, either tube-like or brick-shaped, packed closely together. Under a microscope, they look like a honeycomb. When the tree is felled and the vital fuilds have dried, these tiny air pockets seal, becoming a most perfectly insulated building material. This explains why a log house remains so cool during the summer and why it takes so many days to chill off if left during the winter. It also explains why sounds are absorbed and why music floats so softly through the rooms of a solid timber building. Vapour control is taken care of, too; household moisture is not absorbed to any degree by the log and yet, any which does exist internally will find its own route out as it always did, via the log ends.

Therefore, the tree as it exists naturally is already an almost perfect building material. And for "finish", if the bark has been peeled with care so that no gouging, scarring, or scratching of the wood is allowed to occur, the log will dry to the sort of satiny finish that tempts hands to reach out and stroke it. Do so, for that's how to fully appreciate its smoothness. If, next, the log is washed free of dirt, allowed to dry again, and given a single oiling with boiled linseed oil or Danish oil, the surface becomes not only satin-

smooth but also sufficiently waterproof on the inside to resist household vapour. I know of no sawn, cut, or "finished" wood of any kind, as capable of this--and it is my opinion that a tree is the product of millions of years of tree trial, proven successful. It only remains for us as builders to accord the tree the respect it deserves.

The tree, as an endangered species

It is also good to keep in mind, as we approach the study of solid timber construction, that the log builder is in an enviable position of being able to preserve a part of the relentless harvest of an endangered species.

Under to-day's export-oriented trading conditions, the tree is doomed. Like the buffalo, the trumpeter swan, the sea otter, and the whole sweet-natured legion of beings who have brought swift and

easy profits to people who never cared that such bounty might end, the tree simply cannot grow fast enough or reproduce swiftly enough to survive the toll being taken of them.

It requires at least 100 years to grow a mature tree and up to 500 years for it to reach its maximum growth as shown in the following photos from the British

Columbia Archives. The best forest technology can only speed that process up to a 50-year period. But in the meantime, economic pressures are forcing the logging industry into an almost irresistible trend toward harvesting younger timber, especially if it is close to any road. Industry cannot be held fully at fault, for it is the general public which cries out for

Right: 1895, near Vancouver, British Columbia, this Douglas Fir stood 417 feet tall with 300 feet to its first limbs; circumference at base: 77 feet; butt diameter: 25 feet.

Lower, centre: Douglas Fir circa 1900.

Lower left and lower right: Western Red Cedar.

"employment" and the government must ask industry to set up the conditions for mass employment. Enormous cash profits are needed to establish mills, factories, and the supporting cities. There is little alternative, in such circumstances, but to mow the trees down as if the forests were fields of ripe wheat. And, afterwards, to search out any customer or create any product geared to immediate cash sales. Thus, it might not be entirely tragic if the giant timbers were gone but something splendid remained in their place. But instead we get smouldering moonscapes of stumps and subsoil, because every tree was either trampled or needed to pay the unbelievable costs of the tree shears, forwarders, skidders, loaders, and logging trucks which haul them to the mills. And instead of noble architecture or even a well-housed population, we're more likely to get toilet tissue, newsprint, paper towelling, advertising flyers, fake wallboard, and cardboard cartons . . . and next day, much of that is in the rivers, heaped in land-dumps, or smouldering into the atmosphere. National economic policies which try single-mindedly to create jobs are often bogged down in the notion that the more processes a natural resource is subjected to, the more employment it creates, with greater advantage to all. But higher costs plus less real productivity equals the formula for inflation: less purchasing capability for the ones who need those jobs. Thus many people cannot afford to buy, from their earnings in the industrial workplace, the products they manufacture. Some opt for debt; others choose to build with natural, usually free, materials, such as logs. Those who treasure what timber we still have, are the Conservers, building for tomorrow. There is employment aplenty in this option, as every good 20th century log builder knows. These careful builders may yet write the mighty chapter in Canadian architectural history showing how rare and beautiful logs naturally are, as building material.

Not only is the tree slow-growing, it is also painfully slow to reproduce. It isn't at all like the herbs which can reach maturity and cast seed in one summer — it requires many years of undisturbed growth before the first cones can provide seed. Tree-planting might be argued, as a solution to sustaining the forests but there are many hazards working against it as a completely successful practice. And further, tree-planting lags far behind tree-harvesting. John Walters, director of the University of British Columbia's research forest operations, calls it "The Great Forest Rip-Off", in the December/January 1974 issue of Big Wheel Logging News: "500,000 acres logged per year and 250,000 acres burned per year but only 110,000 acres planted per year!" That's in British Columbia where ½ the provincial budget comes from timber revenues.

Trees have no adequate defence against human encroachment: land-clearing and farming, erosion, chemicals, fires. They have absolutely no defense against highway systems, industrial complexes, power developments, airports, stripmining, and all the housing and blacktopping and shopping-plaza forms of urbinization. But above all, trees cannot possibly continue to exist when these massive profits are needed to support what we call "employment" and when these trees are the raw ingredient upon which the mills, factories, and cities are feeding.

It is important to know that the tree, under these circumstances, is doomed. To build correctly, the log builder must be aware that he still has the priceless opportunity to preserve some trees as architecture. In so doing he will be creating something of perhaps greater longterm social value that he may, at first, appreciate. Certainly I never as fully understood this fact myself as I did when visiting the Grey Nuns' House (shown next) at Saint-Boniface and the Curator explained to me that this four storey building had been hewn of oak. Oak! I could scarcely believe that such timbers had ever existed. But there they were, almost as beautiful after 130 years of seasoning in those walls, as they must have been as trees growing along the banks of the Red River. It was at that moment, I fully realized that the log builder acts as custodian, preserving the best of the logs from an era. Good log buildings may, in the next century, be all that's left of our vanished forests. The Grey Nuns' House is certainly one of the few fragments the nation has left of those oaks that once grew . . . and may never be seen again . . . on the Red River in Manitoba.

"I wish all to know that I do not propose to sell any part of my country, nor will I have the whites cutting our timber along the rivers, more especially the oak. I am particularly fond of the little groves of oak trees. I love to look at them, because they endure the wintry storm and the summer's heat, and — not unlike ourselves — seem to flourish by them."

— Chief Sitting Bull (Tatanka Yotanka)

timber over the longterm, despite the fact that it appears to be the slowest. I know of forests where major logging had been undertaken, over the same terrain, every 10 years . . . until the big yellow machines moved in and mowed everything down in the clearcut method which, in my opinion, requires a minimum of 100 years to recuperate. Or as one old logger said, more realistically, "Let's face it, it's gone forever. Nobody will log here again."

Consider another example of making the optimum use of timber: one logging truckload of logs can sustain only a few hours' activity in the mill or plywood plant . . . but a truckload of good logs can provide a year's highly paid work for the log builder who, furthermore, creates a product of far higher market value. And without soil pollution, air pollution, or water pollution. Most of the income goes to the men doing the work rather that to pay for machinery. What's more, the log builder didn't need a foreign investor to set him up in an industrial complex or government to supply him with a city or urban services. He initiates secondary work for those who make blacksmith's hardware or leaded glass windows, as well as for carvers and stonemasons, and for the plumbers, electricians, floor layers, and so on. The log builder is in a privileged position, really: a free man, handsomely paid, engaged in healthful work, valued in the community.

But any privilege, to endure, must be based in social responsibility. An intelligent society will not long tolerate the man who tries to cream off truck loads of resources for questionable use. Therefore, *how he builds* is of special concern. If the ancient and honoured craft is to survive he'll shape and fit logs

Interior wall of hewn oak, Grey Nuns' House.

Three conservation practices for the log builder

Leaving aside corporate and industrial problem-solving, three methods of forest conservation are of special concern to the log builder. Under the broad general aim of making optimum use of timber resources, he should be particularly aware of (1) how he logs ... (2) how he builds ... (3) what he builds.

The log builder is fortunate if he can go

into the woods to pick out the trees he'll be working with. This way he obtains the size and the conformity of log he prefers. He also gets the trees out undamaged and a fine set of building logs not gouged, scraped, shattered, or scarred by machinery is a great beginning for a house. Most important, however, is the opportunity of leaving an undisturbed forest able, within only a few years more, to provide its next crop. Selective logging makes this possible. Loggers familiar with selective logging methods believe it to be the most profitable and efficient way of sustaining the supply of

The room of "The Order of Good Cheer" as it was in 1605. Note size of knee braces.

Roof trussing as built by ships' carpenters in Champlain's "Habitation", Port Royal, Nova Scotia.

France not only encouraged excellent builders but also took care to preserve their architectural drawings, thus making it possible to rebuild in exact detail such significant structures as Champlain's "Habitation" (shown above) just as it was in 1605, Port Royal, as well as part of the Fortress of Louisbourg, 1720-45.

as tightly as ever ships' timbers were fitted. His artistic judgment will put fine logs to their finest use, as did Champlain's carpenters. He'll meet or exceed every aspect of any national building code. Let the log builder view this high standard of work as straight economic dollars and sense. Or let him build beautifully as an act of faith in the future, or of homage to the past. Whatever his motivation, the front-rank log builder knows that the road to excellence is the only way to go if we

are to safeguard this great privilege of building with logs. If we succeed in combining productivity with elegance and excellence, society sees that it's good business, working with nature. If we fail, it helps convince society that mills and factories can do everything better. In my opionion, a great responsibility rests upon the 20th century log builder . . . for he's one of the rare industries working to full employment, creating a valuable product, employing many secondary spin-off

trades, and doing all of this under modern conditions, by all the urban and suburban rules, yet he's still working hand-in-glove with nature in a non-polluting, humanistic way. He is one of the real trail-blazers of the future . . . if he holds true to his own beliefs and methods, and especially to his own colleagues.

Therefore, *what he builds*, can be safely assumed in these 1980's, will be nothing but strong, handsome log buildings. But let me tell you: this safe assumption was hard-won. It represents a most significant milestone in the developmental sequence of the modern log building renaissance.

The Lawg Caybun concept in building

When BUILDING WITH LOGS was first written, early in 1971, the word "cabin" appeared nowhere in it. Certainly, I was aware that log cabins existed, both literally and linguistically. But as I myself did not use the term and did not live in, build, or teach about cabins, it was my uncomplicated belief that the term had nothing to do with me or my book. It was an error of omission. For several years, my students and I endured that double-edged sword: praise for my log cabins, compliments on my log cabin book. The more I ignored it, the more the term seemed to thrive . . . like a weed unplucked. So the 4th, 5th, and 6th editions addressed the question. I showed how the term had originated and why the term had come to have 'less of its original meaning as shelter for the poor, the oppressed, or the actual slaves . . . and to have more and more meaning as an exalted political symbol of possible upward social mobility.

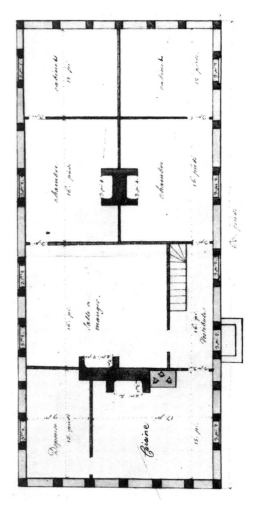

Profil et Elevation du batiment...
en Charpente pour le Logement du Lieutenant du Roy
1733

French military engineers and draftsmen were one of the most skilled professional classes of the time. Plans they produced routinely were carefully drawn and coloured and are characterized by their meticulous detail as well as artistic embellishment. It is not generally recognized how much we owe to the French engineers for our visual record of Louisbourg,

and much of North America. The drawings made throughout New France show how common was this technical expertise and how often it resulted in a superlative record of buildings.... Louisbourg was large enough to have commercial, military, residential districts... public buildings were monumental. Where else in the North

American colonies during that period (early 1700's) were structures comparable in size and concept to the Casernes of Louisbourg or the Artillery Barracks in Quebec City ...? Did any activity elsewhere result in a body of maps and plans comparable to those created by the French?

- Bulletin of the Assoc. Preservation Technol. Vol. IV, #1-2, 1972.

The Lartigue house being rebuilt to look as it did in 1735 when it belonged to the Fortress of Louisbourg, Cape Breton Island.

Right: 1735 houseplans for a similar home

Log builders laugh now, when they recall the old battles waged and won. It took a while. A great many people wrote and I especially appreciated those letters from the U.S.A. thanking me for making the difference clear, between the politics and the building concept, and saying they saw improved results just from that new understanding.

So in these enlightened times, few people mistake a house for a cabin. They know that we are not cabin-builders. Just to be on the safe side, and for those who did not see the previous editions, it may be prudent to go over the main arguments against that cabin concept.

My premise was that the term, "log cabin", had done greater injury to the proper development of log buildings than had all the bark beetles, termites, dry rot, lightening strikes, mildew, uncaring tenants, or bad workmanship in all history.

The log cabin term has no legitimate place in Canadian history. The French from earliest Champlain (Port Royal, 1605) used logs magnificently. The British also held a firm conviction in maintaining the timber framing techniques they had always known. And even when such groups as the United Empire Loyalists arrived from the United States as refugees, they quickly contrived shelters of log which they then called "shanties" or "huts" but never "cabins" . . . they knew too well its slave connotation. Later when they built a family home, usually of log, it was called a house. Naturally. Shown above is a typically neat hewn log home of 19th century Ontario. It is the kind of home to which settlers often brought, at great pains, at least one object of great beauty: a piano, a set of fine

china, a carved bed . . . to which they pointed with pride, hoping for the day when they could furnish their entire household to that standard. The above home succeeded in doing that.

I had found, too, that the cabin concept was crippling for students who could not be unlocked from the grip of that stereotype. Those who imagined log building construction to be a survey of rustic, rough shelters had destroyed most of their opportunity to learn how to build well. Good concept is the prerequisite for a builder. It defines any project.

One of the most dramatic log homes built by any of my students was done by an English teacher and his Librarian wife, neither of whom had had any previous building experience of any sort. But they did have intelligence, stamina, ambition, and above all a tremendous appreciation

of what solid timber could be made to do. They could relate whatever they heard, saw, or practised in class to this expanded concept. As a result, their home has impact. To enter its main hall is to stop, struck by the many expressions of openness, height, light, warmth, colours, spatial arrangements, and much more which is difficult to articulate . . . something very much to do with the richness of the human heritage, timeless and undaunted just so long as it is valued.

Finally to illustrate further the power of good concept, I described the lady who willingly did enough homework in 1972 for me to realize fully the consequences of a log cabin stereotype. She asked my advice: would two fireplaces (and no furnace) provide adequate heat throughout a Prairie winter in the 61 ft. by 44 ft. "log cabin" she and her husband proposed to

wilderness camp, the summer cottage, the mountain lookout . . . but these temporary, substandard structures are unworthy of solid timber construction. Rather, let the conservationists be the first to pitch tents or to build with plywood, insisting that those 40 or 50 trees be left to grow until someone can carefully craft them into centuries-enduring buildings.

The log builder is enjoying what could be the dying hours of a privileged profession, if care is not taken. If society is to allow him -- and perhaps even to encourage him -- to continue working in a medium so fast disappearing from even our most favoured regions, the log builder must lead the way in woods conservation. Let us resolve, therefore, to take sufficient time to log selectively wherever possible . . . to work carefully . . . and to produce log buildings of the highest order of beauty and excellence. It can be no other way, if we hope to continue building with logs.

build. It was an important point, she explained, because they hoped to raise a family and live forever in that 2,684 square foot dream home but wanted it to be "as authentic as possible", i.e., no heat. She intended sawing barrels in half to serve as appropriate living room furniture and thanked me for my efforts "to bring this lifestyle back into existence". I couldn't imagine what she meant . . . but suspected the Lawg Caybun stereotype was at work degrading her blueprint and threatening to render her home "authentic-awful". The best help I thought I could give her was remedial reading. She was a good student. "No, I didn't notice that you never used the word 'cabin' anywhere in your book," replied a somewhat subdued correspondent. "I did as you instructed and looked the word up in a dictionary. It in no way describes the structure in which we plan to live. It is also true that I would never have referred to it as a 'cabin' had we been planning to build a brick or plywood structure. In fact, since you pointed out its meaning, I have formed a passionate dislike for the word . . ." She needed no other help than this change of concept. With the image corrected, she was easily able to make the necessary heating improvements to her houseplan as well as to upgrade the interior furnishings to chairs more appropriate to a permanent residence of that scope and significance. The lesson left me indebted, however, for it was the first time I saw clearly illustrated the devastating influence of Lawg Caybunism, thanks to her patient study. And it was this lady who brought to my attention the way in which Shakespeare had used the word "cabin" to mean unhappy confinement, as in MacBeth:

"But now I am Cabin'd, cribb'd, confin'd, bound in to saucy doubts and fears . . ."

That pioneers of bygone centuries wasted timber on some small, bad buildings is undeniable. But they worked to survive, the trees were being felled and burned to create fields, and, besides, they knew no better. We do . . . and so logs, in this day and age, ought to be the unthinkable material for "cabin"-making. Let there be an end to the travesty of mimicking the worst that pioneers did while ignoring their best. I am especially sad when conservationists and wilderness buffs, those pollution-fighting resource-protecting outdoors people, are to be found leading the parade of "cabin"-lovers. I agree, there is a special joy in the

Tools

The tie hackers and shake splitters who moved into the bush to work the winter, not so very many years ago, were said to have had their sawmills on their backs. This was true, inasmuch as they could build their own accommodation for the winter with the tools they could carry: a double-bitted axe, a broad axe, a crosscut saw or framesaw, an auger bit (the handle to made in the woods), plus a piece of sheet metal for the stove and a small packet of shingle nails. This, along with a bedroll and a few days' supply of groceries, set a man up in business.

Conditions in the woods have changed greatly . . . for loggers. But for the lone woodsman, the basic tools -- with the exception of the chain saw -- have changed little. Because your building is going to be larger and of a more permanent nature, there is need for a somewhat expanded list of tools. The most important of these, in addition to a basic set of carpenter's tools, is a log scriber, a peeling spud, and log dogs.

A pair of good scribers is essential, for these are the key to measuring for perfectly fitted logs. Their helpfulness cannot be overestimated.

Many types and designs of scribers

have been made, generally by the person who expects to use them. So, purely as a guide, I have included in a later section of this book when we come to walls and the actual use of the scriber, a dimensioned diagram of the ones which I have found to be most successful. My favourite ones were made from an old chain saw blade. But scribers can also be made from a heavy pair of machinist's or tinsmith's dividers and I also use a pair like this, fitted up with a level which is custom-made for the Mackie School. By means of this level, it is possible to see at all times whether or not the instrument is being held in the correct perpendicular position. For marking, they are fitted with an indelible pencil which puts a clear mark on any log, green, wet, or dry.

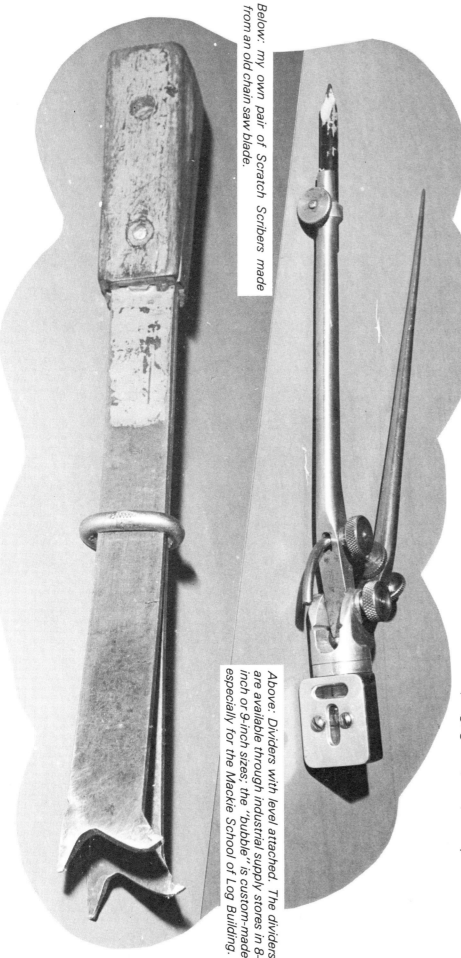

Below: my own pair of Scratch Scribers made from an old chain saw blade.

Above: Dividers with level attached. The dividers are available through industrial supply stores in 8-inch or 9-inch sizes; the "bubble" is custom-made especially for the Mackie School of Log Building.

LOG DOGS

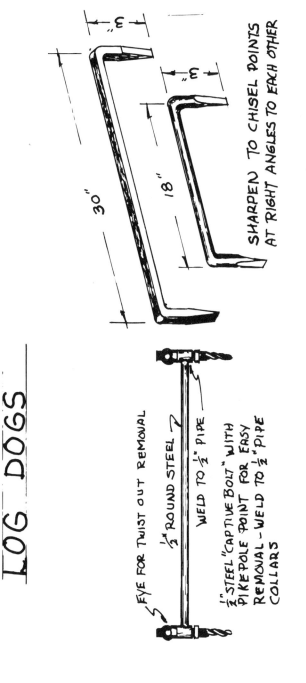

30"

3"

18"

3"

SHARPEN TO CHISEL POINTS
AT RIGHT ANGLES TO EACH OTHER

EYE FOR TWIST OUT REMOVAL

½" ROUND STEEL

WELD TO ½" PIPE

1" STEEL "CAPTIVE BOLT" WITH
PIKEPOLE POINT FOR EASY
REMOVAL — WELD TO ½" PIPE
COLLARS

Scribers should be strong enough to be able to cut or mark a good clear line in the log. They must also be handy enough to fit close to the log on the corners. They should have a way to set the distance between the points firmly, without danger of slipping. "Fin" type scribers can be made by a blacksmith and very good ones of this kind can be made from a No. 4 coyote trap, which has the added advantage of keeping the trap from being any further danger to the coyotes. Cut the eyes of the spring through at right angles to the spring so that they have a fishtail cutting edge. Heat and squeeze the spring to a sharper bend and put a keeper around it. In use, the cutting points are set at the desired distance with a small block of wood and then the keeper is driven up tightly.

PEELING SPUD

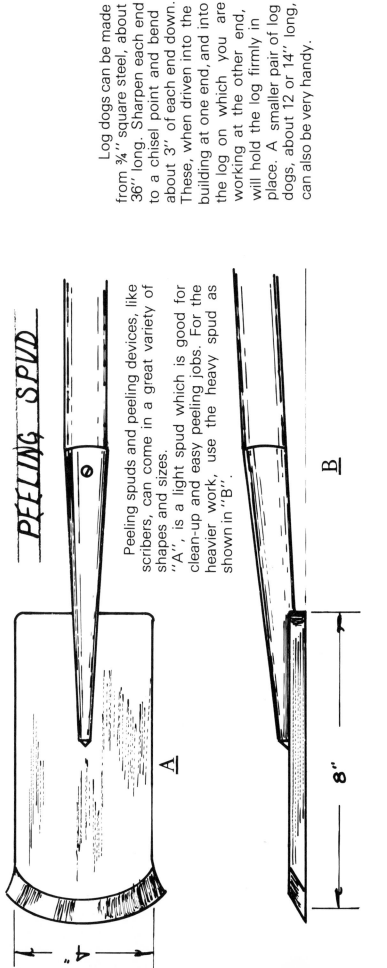

A

B

4"

8"

Peeling spuds and peeling devices, like scribers, can come in a great variety of shapes and sizes. "A", is a light spud which is good for clean-up and easy peeling jobs. For the heavier work, use the heavy spud as shown in "B".

Log dogs can be made from ¾" square steel, about 36" long. Sharpen each end to a chisel point and bend about 3" of each end down. These, when driven into the building at one end, and into the log on which you are working at the other end, will hold the log firmly in place. A smaller pair of log dogs, about 12 or 14" long, can also be very handy.

13

The tool that can accomplish a great deal in a short time is a gasoline-powered chain saw. Because it is noisy and smoky is not enough to recommend that a good axe be used in its place, but experience has indicated that the chain saw is perhaps even more dangerous than was

originally understood. In addition to the immediate dangers of coming in contact with the chain, there is increasing evidence that high vibration levels are causing serious circulatory problems. Vibratory White Finger, or Raynaud's Disease, is the occupational hazard to be feared by all who hold a vibrating tool in their hands, be that a pneumatic drill, a shoe repair lathe, or a chain saw. It is far more widespread than one, at first, might imagine. This, in part, is due to the fact that the initial symptoms appear so trivial: a slight tingling in the finger tips, followed later by a numbness, then by a distinctive white colour which is the sure danger signal that the blood supply has been temporarily cut off. If exposure continues, the damage continues until the fingers cannot be made to button up clothing or pick up small objects. Unless the operator stops using the vibrating tool, the final result is gangrene for which the only cure is amputation. Another chain saw related occupational hazard is loosely termed "sawdust asthma" caused by the extremely fine sawdust particles from dry or treated wood. Breathing this - in my own case, for even 5-minute periods, now -- brings on this bronchial disorder. At the end of 1977, when I had taught 15 short courses from the University of British Columbia's Pacific shores, to Seafoam County, Nova Scotia, I was coughing blood at the end of some lectures. It was two years before I was willing to risk this level of exposure again . . . and I am doing some Eastern seaboard teaching, now, with the aid of an assistant. My work at the Mackie School of Log Building is similarly curtailed to lectures and specific demonstrations. I have found the simple cure for both these serious occupational hazards: the axe. I

use an axe, now, as much as possible.

I don't really favour one brand of saw above another because almost any saw gives good service if it is looked after

correctly. But, in general, a very big saw is too dangerous to handle in high or awkward places on a building, and the itty bitty saws developed for Cheechakos are, in spite of the manufacturers' claims, usually good for nothing. Use a moderate size saw of 4 to 4.5 cubic inch displacement and with a relatively high cutting speed. Bar length should be 16 to 20 inches. The shorter bar is good for working on the building but the longer bar is needed for falling trees. Some saws have a high noise characteristic and, out

Axes should be kept sharp. File into the bit, "cutting" the file with the axe. A good handle on the file prevents cuts if the file slips. Start filing a distance back from the edge and work out to the edge. This will keep the blade slim and parabolic in shape. Too thin an edge will chip or bend, but an axe must be sharp, as a dull axe can slip or glance off the wood.

The owner of a good 2-inch auger is lucky for this is not an easy tool to find. The only care it nees is protection of the edges from gravel, dirt, or nails. Grease it well before storage to prevent rust. In use, a hand auger should not be expected to bore through more than one log at a time...unless it is very long, it will jam up with chips and, once taken out of the cut, it is hard to start again. Bridge augers will drill deeper, particularly if power driven.

Holes may also be cut with a gouge type of chisel. This chisel has a long curved blade and is sharpened on the inside. It should have a heavy shank so it may be driven with a hammer. I first saw this type of drill among the tools used for making Red River carts, shown in the Duck Lake museum in Saskatchewan. Nowadays, even as in the 1800's, this tool would have to made by a blacksmith.

Gouge type of chisel which could be used for making round holes.

instead of the usual 35° . . . this causes the saw to cut slower, but it will produce a smoother cut on a notch and the chain will rip faster when doing a lateral groove.

POOR   DOUBTFUL   GOOD

Choose an axe handle with a good clean edge grain, as at right above.

Axes are, to a large extent, a matter of personal preference. I no longer use the double-bitted axes because they have proven too dangerous where there are several people around a work-site. A number of good axes have come onto the market since the demand has increased so dramatically in the last several years. These are the 4 to 5½ lb. axes with excellent finish and balance. Good handles are also available, if one is careful enough in selection. Choose a 28' to 30'' handle that has a good clean edge grain, is made of hickory without sap wood, and of course is straight.

of respect for your eardrums, should be avoided. And, of course, you'll be looking for vibration-damping characteristics in any saw you buy, plus the absolutely essential Chain Brake which stops the action instantly in case of kickback. As some protection against ear and eye damage, I recommend the wearing of a crash helmet with full plastic screen covering the face. There are padded gloves on the market, too, which help a little in protecting the hands from White Finger disease.

To look after a chain saw, observe two rules: mix the gasoline and oil properly; and keep the chain sharp, properly tensioned and well oiled. The manufacturer will recommend a mixing proportion of gasoline and oil for the particular saw . . . this may be 16 parts gasoline to one part oil, or it may be as high as 50 parts gasoline to one part oil. The use of synthetic oils will again affect this ratio.

Whatever the mix, pour a portion of the carefully measured original volume back into a smaller container. Add the oil to this smaller amount. And mix throroughly. When mixing is complete, pour this mix back into the larger amount and stir again. If some oil remains in the small container, which may happen in cold weather, pour some of the mix back again until all the oil is suspended in the gasoline. When pouring the mix into the gasoline tank of the saw, use a strainer funnel and be careful to avoid having sawdust or snow enter the tank.

Chain filing and tensioning are best done in accordance with the manufacturer's recommendation for the saw. I prefer to file the teeth at a lesser horizontal angle than is generally used for bucking logs. I reduce this angle to 25°